Cobwebs
And
Ugly Wallpaper

A Collection of Short Essays
About Your Life

Second Edition

Anthony Ferraioli, M.D.

This little book is dedicated to you, the reader, for your interest and struggles.

It is also dedicated with great joy and love to my children and to yours....

And, of course, to my darling wife, whom I love.

Finally, a special heartfelt thanks and acknowledgement to the previous generations and their own struggles.

Contents

Introduction

First things first.

And that is this: it is definitely NOT essential that you read this Introduction.

If you like, you can just go ahead and pick out some interesting sounding Chapters (Essays) and enjoy them. I've kept them "short and sweet" for you. Follow what interests you and read with your heart, and you'll already have gotten the point of this book, even in one sitting.

Now for the rest.

Through my work with people I've come to believe more and more that the main issues of our lives are NOT unlimited or too complex to address. In fact, I have seen a certain set of main themes develop over and over again in people's therapy work with me over the years.

This is what prompted me to compile this series of short, plainly written essays, which I have written over time to keep track of some of these main themes. I present them here, all in one place, for you to read and share with the important people in your life.

The idea for this book originally came from my wish to give my new patients a *starting point* from which to build in their sessions with me and in their private reflections.

I wanted most of all to begin to leave, in writing, a direct explanation of what people have taught me are some very important issues for anyone who wishes to live a better life, including my own children.

I've kept the chapters purposely short and the wording straightforward and simple. It is important for me to emphasize that the point here is not to treat each topic exhaustively, but to *begin* the discussion.

What is joy? How can we humans manage to not feel depressed or anxious in life, instead finding joy and energy and a zest for living. How can we get to a point in life where we feel that time flies *all the time*, and that the most serious issue is that life is too short?

Well, the short story (very, very short) is this: *people are happiest when they live lives that are as close as possible to what their true or inner selves want.*

So what's a *true or inner self?*

With my patients, I always describe the true self as that part of us that "knows all". It observes us, and keeps track of how close or far we come to expressing who we really are in our lives. This includes pursuing what we really want to do in the world as well as how we really want to interact with others and how we are feeling in any given circumstance.

My view of a person's true or inner self is that part of them that really, really knows what they want and don't want at any given moment, including in the short, medium, and long terms in life.

Some other thoughts on the true or inner self:

It's the part of each of us that feels like saying something to someone when we've been wronged by them.

It's the part that knows what kind of work or hobbies it likes to do, with whom it wants to spend time, and how it wants to be treated or feels it should treat others.

It's the part of us that tells us *how to work* and *how to love* (you'll see more on this in the "Bicycle of Life" Chapter.)

It's the part that keeps track of how true or untrue we are to ourselves, and ultimately controls how good or bad we will feel because of it.

So, what happens when we do not "obey" the true self over and over again with time?

Well, when we're not living our lives as much as possible by the will of our true selves, we are prone to *internal conflict*, which ultimately leads to depression, mood swings, anxiety, etc. At the very least, it leads to less than optimal living.

Here is a simple illustration. If someone is being abusive towards you in some way and you do not at least *attempt* to do *something* to protect yourself, you can be sure that you will eventually have a buildup of emotions which will not be healthy for you and which can ultimately lead to depression, anxiety, loss of energy and motivation, self-loathing, etc.

When we cannot, because of fear, guilt, shame, etc., say what needs to be said or behave the way we really feel would be most appropriate (including protecting ourselves and our interests, such as, in some cases, our children), chances are that we've come up against an internal conflict. It is then likely that, instead of doing or saying what we really feel, we will say or behave in a way that feels less threatening to us, even though it may not be exactly what we mean and it may not even be healthy for us. This is the basis of a "defense mechanism". In some cases this process occurs subconsciously and we *don't even recognize it at all!*

Without getting into too much jargon, our defense mechanisms can range from the more healthy (ie. using humor, suppression, altruism, anticipation), to the less healthy (ie. using denial, projection, passive aggression, and *acting out*.)

So, forgetting for a moment about all this talk of *internal conflicts* and *defense mechanisms*, let's have another illustration of how the true or inner self works. And let's use a very silly example, one that I use quite often in my office.

If the checkout person at the supermarket gives you paper bags and you really wanted plastic and you choose to accept paper instead, your true self sits there and keeps track of that failure to protect its interests, believe it or not.

As I say to my patients, "the body never forgets", meaning the mind or subconscious mind remembers these things, no matter how seemingly trivial, and they WILL add up and come back later as depression, anxiety, obsessive thoughts or behaviors, self-loathing, guilt, low energy, aches and pains, decreased concentration, etc.

Another example: if a neighbor or friend's child, or anyone really, even a teacher or other presumably well-meaning adult, repeatedly hurts your child (even in subtle emotional ways) and you neglect saying something to them for fear of how they'll take it, you will have betrayed not only your own true self interests, but even those of your child.

Believe me, these things add up not only for us but for our children too, potentially affecting their self esteem, moods, and even who they choose to be with and what they do with their lives.

Same thing goes for spousal relationships, friendships, and even with regards to our relationships with our parents.

Part of expressing one's true or inner self in life is to attempt to set proper *boundaries* with people, and even with various institutions, believe it or not.

For example, if you're finding that the institution you work for tends to treat people in a "use them up and throw them out" sort of way, you've encountered what might be called a *narcissistic system*, in which the nurturing and fair treatment of the individual is not a primary goal.

Some *families* are quite "narcissistic" in this way, meaning that the focus is not on emotionally nurturing the children but on something else (like a parent's health problems or career, or maintaining a certain image in the community, or staying ahead of the neighbors, etc.)

You'd be surprised how many families and institutions are like this, including (and maybe especially) some very well respected ones that are just not healthy for the people in them.

So, in summary, living a joyful, energized life includes attempting to stay true to one's self, including protecting one's interests, pursuing what one wants in the world, and expressing one's truth in interactions with others, including setting appropriate boundaries. But what else?

Well, in short, it also involves avoiding unhealthy *substitution activities* which temporarily soothe us when we are feeling the pain of loneliness, sadness, anger, humiliation, confusion, or feeling "stuck". For example, people drink, use drugs, have sex, drive fast cars, jump out of airplanes, and lots of other things that provide a temporary escape or relief from unpleasant feelings. Some might refer to these activities as "acting out" behaviors.

Of course, some of these things can also be enjoyed in a healthy manner as well. I'm only talking about when we use them as coping mechanisms for dealing with life's harder emotions and situations.

I believe that each time we substitute a behavior or activity in order to avoid the anxiety or confusion of the moment, we actually drive a wedge between ourselves and our true, inner selves at that time.

For example, if I'm feeling anxious or lonely or guilty or sad, or even if I don't know WHAT I'm feeling, but I instantly choose a substitute activity or behavior to feel better, I will ultimately feel worse afterwards. Then I'll be even more anxious, confused, guilty, upset, etc. than before. Ultimately depression increases and hopelessness and feeling "stuck" increases. (You'll see more on this in the Chapter called "Cobwebs and Ugly Wallpaper.")

Net result: we are even more removed from knowing what we really feel, really want, really don't want, etc. In other words, further from feeling our truest selves.

Learning to bear and work through tough times and tough emotions without immediately trying to escape them is a very *adult* way of living, loving, and working. It's what brings us closer to feeling the joy, energy, and power of being close to our truest selves. And it's what gives us a level of *command of ourselves as emotionally competent adults.* Certainly, as you'll see in this book, those around us, including and maybe especially children, will also benefit greatly from our growing emotional competence.

In any case, these issues are sort of the tip of the iceberg of what gets discussed in my work with my private patients, as well as the things I continue to think about regularly and continue to refine, write about, and talk about each day.

I've written them down in this book for you.

So, what follows in the upcoming chapters are very simple, very short explanations of some of these topics, the ones I find most important and the ones I most want you to know about. I've included just enough information to *start* the discussion and to help you begin reflecting with yourself and those around you, including perhaps with your own therapist or maybe with your spouse or family.

You'll notice that I use lots of what I call analogies, though I'm sure that some may call them metaphors, all with pretty silly but memorable names to help you incorporate some of these concepts into your life *now*.

Believe it or not, the essays in this little book form a cohesive whole, which I think is best appreciated if it is read several times over here and there when time allows, in no particular order.

And I feel that the true beauty of how these topics weave together is that they help form a core of understanding about how we live, love, work, get hurt, and heal.

Enjoy and,

Thanks for your interest,

Anthony Ferraioli, M.D.

chapter

1

"LVAC"

I made up this mnemonic for my patients as an aide in remembering how to interact with others, especially if you have children or a spouse, but really with just about anyone.

I believe it is quite powerful, and it has far-reaching implications, as I'll explain later.

So here it is: LVAC— "L" is for Listen, "V" is for Validate, "A" is for Ask, and "C" is for Comment.

It is important that you do these things in the order of the mnemonic. For example, if you are speaking with your significant other, you would first Listen to what they are trying to tell you, then you would Validate them by making an empathetic comment or sound to let them know you have heard them and are thinking about what they are saying.

If you've done these two things, the third is usually less necessary, but by all means **A**sk questions to clarify and further show your interest in what the other person is saying. Then, and ONLY then, should you **C**omment on what they are saying to you.

The problem is that most people do LVAC *in reverse*!

If you begin to observe yourself when speaking with others, whether in person or by phone, you will no doubt begin to notice that you too do the LVAC mnemonic in reverse.

In other words, like most people, you might Comment first, then Ask questions, and, if time allows or your attention is still focused, maybe you might make an empathetic comment or two, but many people leave this out entirely.

The result of the "backwards LVAC" is leaving the other person feeling that you really were not placing them first when they needed you for a few moments.

For children, the "backwards LVAC" is even worse, as it is only by using the LVAC technique in the proper order that we allow our children *the* major childhood opportunity to *define themselves emotionally* (more on this later.)

By simply following the LVAC mnemonic we discipline ourselves to give the other person the first priority, attention, and focus, for just a few minutes. With children this can be especially powerful and rewarding, as they learn to come first to you with their deepest, most troubling concerns or emotional conflicts because they feel nurtured with LVAC.

I've had many patients whose teenage children began to withhold information from them, getting secretive about matters of secret "crushes"; or, potentially more harmful, about alcohol, drugs, or sex.

For these families, the LVAC mnemonic helps create an environment where the child finds themselves with a ready, non-self-centered, and "emotionally competent" parent to go to as a first resource with problems, rather than having to hide things or numb themselves with drugs or other temporary fixes, including cutting, for emotional pain relief.

As mentioned a minute ago, another key point about LVAC is that, by doing it with our children, *we allow them to define themselves emotionally.*

What does this mean?

Well, if you're dealing with a child and you do the steps to LVAC (Listen, Validate, Ask, and Comment), even without realizing it you have just helped that child not only deal with the current situation, but you've also helped guide them to the more long-term goal of understanding themselves better and more fully.

I truly believe that no approach to our children is more powerful and more fulfilling, none.

And, what's more, you don't have to immediately come up with the answer for them! You "simply" LVAC your way through the situation with them, and the process itself often makes the situation better, or at least bearable, for them.

It works, trust me.

Think about it: if you, like most people, do the LVAC backwards (ie., Comment first), you have now passed on your own "opinion", "conclusion", or "anxiety" (ie. your "comment") onto the child.

Yes folks, this is how we pass down our own neurotic conflicts and anxieties to our kids; generation after generation after generation, etc…because we tend to comment first, instead of Listening, Validating, Asking clarifying questions, and *then* Commenting if necessary.

To stop this cycle and to give your children the maximum in personal power and inner peace in adulthood, it's simple: LVAC!

I believe with all my heart that this one simple technique can make the difference between a good life and a great one for them.

Quick example of the *wrong, or comment first* approach:

Little Johnny: "Mom, I just went over to Billy's house and he took away my new truck and won't give it back."

Mom: "Johnny, how many times have I told you to stay away from Billy? Now you get over there and get your truck back or you're not getting any more new trucks ever again!"

The only thing accomplished here is the communication, consciously or unconsciously, of Mom's agenda: her expression to her child of her being overwhelmed by the situation with her own anger and anxiety. Benefit for the child: minimal, unless you count that her expressing her own limits in frustration tolerance are now passed onto him as his limits too.

Now for the LVAC version:

Little Johnny: "Mom, I just went over to Billy's house and he took away my new truck and won't give it back."

Mom: Listening to the above first, then Validating with "Oh, I'm sorry about your truck honey…", then Asking, "Can you tell me what happened?"

Notice, the Listening step allows the child to communicate all that he wishes to without fear of being punished, shamed, or humiliated by the parent.

Next, the Validating step allows him to feel whatever he really is feeling (maybe fear? shame? anger? etc.) and also allows him to accept these feelings and not try to ward them off immediately or run away from them by forming some kind of defense mechanism against them. (Also see the Introduction to this book for further discussion of the meaning of a defense mechanism.) Keep in mind that any strong defense mechanisms he forms now, will likely limit him in life later. (See Chapter entitled "We Fail with the Heart, Not the Brain.")

Finally, the Asking step helps the child to clarify his own thoughts and feelings on the situation at hand, instead of having this process short-circuited by the parent's comments.

I've left out the Comment step intentionally in the above example to illustrate how, in so many cases, if the first three steps are done well, it really becomes unnecessary to comment much at all, or perhaps only as an afterthought. This also benefits the parent insomuch as you don't have to immediately take a stand, come up with *the answer*, or get carried away with your own anxiety, anger, fear, etc.

As you might imagine regarding LVAC in your other relationships, including marital, the technique adds a richness and a mutual empathy which soothes and nurtures each of you, since, more than likely, nobody took the time and effort to "LVAC" with you or your spouse (most likely because they didn't know how) when you guys were kids. (Take a look at the Chapter entitled "Marriage Part One.")

chapter

2

"The Bicycle of Life"

This is a major topic which many people find useful to explore. The idea here is that if it is true that an indicator of mental health is the ability to work and to love, then it is worthwhile to examine how we work and love in our lives.

If, as we saw in the last chapter, most of us did not receive enough of the LVAC process in childhood, then finding our true selves through what we like, don't like, want, and don't want in terms of *work* and *love*, represents a second opportunity to define or re-find the self, this time in adulthood.

This is great news by the way, because it means that even when we were not given the opportunity in childhood to be Listened to, Validated, Asked to clarify feelings, and *then* given Comments or opinions from our caregivers, we can *still* find our way back to who we really are by later examining our work lives and our relationships (ie. love) in adulthood!

To help people with this I made up a "bicycle" analogy and it goes like this: one wheel of the bike represents love, the other work. For most people, if one or the other wheel is a bit "wobbly" in their lives, they can usually rely on the stability of the other and continue to at least survive everyday life. However, for many it's not that easy, for either both wheels are a bit wobbly, or one wobbles *a lot*.

Again, the key here is that these two wheels of the bicycle (work and love) are *the* major *opportunities* we really have in adulthood to learn more about our true inner selves.

Let's start with work. For perhaps a minority of people I speak with, the work they do everyday, paid or unpaid, truly gives them joy. In other words, their work really does sustain them, is part of who they are, and they usually have good if not great feelings about it.

For these lucky people, their work helps orient their lives and also lends their lives a pace or momentum, gives them a healthy sense of being good at something, and helps feed their self esteem and sense of competence in the world.

When all else seems to be caving in on them, their work in the world helps keep them afloat.

But, for the great majority, their work does not add to their health, but instead challenges it daily. If there is one thing I advise people about it is this: unless there is absolutely no choice, we must strive to find and do what has true meaning to ourselves in our work or we will eventually suffer the consequences in terms of stress, exhaustion, burnout, and, ultimately for many, anxiety and depression.

I believe that work provides an outlet for the expression of our true selves, and that, as such, it can provide a way to feel validated and accepted in the world rather than contribute to a feeling of daily struggle and conflict.

The other "bicycle wheel", love, represents another opportunity in which we can find validation and expression of our true selves in the world.

When we work towards increased emotional intimacy in our relationships, we cultivate something we can cling to when other aspects of life seem to close in on us.

A key to maximizing the love wheel of life is the LVAC technique discussed in Chapter 1. The LVAC technique is a major way we can increase our emotional intimacy with our loved ones, whether they be our children, our spouses, or our friends and acquaintances.

Also, the Chapters entitled "Marriage Part One" and "Marriage Part Two" may be interesting to take a look at, even if you're not married.

There is no doubt that the love wheel can be just as potent, if not more so, than the work one, on the bicycle of life.

chapter

3 "Cobwebs and Ugly Wallpaper"

Often when talking about escapism with my patients, I'll use the "cobwebs" and "ugly wallpaper" analogies.

First, the cobwebs.

The cobwebs represent the unpleasant emotions we are trying to escape in the first place. These may be anxiety, fear, boredom, anger, confusion, loneliness, shame, humiliation, guilt, etc., or any combination of these.

The way the "cobweb" analogy works is this: when we are feeling tempted to do something to escape unpleasant feelings; something which may not be healthy for us but would most certainly feel good for the short term (like drinking, spending, having affairs, etc.), we begin to do two things.

First, we escape for the short term but actually add to our ultimate misery by creating not less, but MORE "cobwebs" in our lives. So what does this mean?

It means that instead of getting true relief from our initial misery, we have actually further clouded our vision (with more cobwebs) of what we *should* be doing by distracting ourselves with whatever escape we just took. *So now we're back from the escape and feeling even worse and more confused, agitated, lonely, hopeless, etc. (more cobwebs.)*

For example: if you really want to go out and buy something for yourself that you perhaps really can't afford right now, but oh the temptation of it is so strong, and you are just convinced that you will feel better after you buy it, there's another side to that coin. (By the way, this is sort of similar to the temptation to drink, do drugs, or other things so many people struggle with every day to escape life's pain.)

What if you go ahead and buy it? Now, you've channeled energy and focus, (not to mention time and money) into shopping for and buying whatever it was that was going to make you feel better. Now if you hadn't done that, what do you think you might have done?

Forget the money for a moment, and just think about the time and energy. Would you have gotten some exercise maybe? Spent time with the kids perhaps? Had some peaceful, unstructured time to just "be"?

But after "returning" from the escape there's no way to find out where your day would have gone had you not tried to escape it—you're now back to square one with no new knowledge of yourself or your life, and your pain is still there (cobwebs.)

There is no doubt that by constantly searching for the next thing (or the same things) to provide short term happiness or relief from boredom, loneliness, etc., we ultimately shortchange ourselves by stealing time and energy away from ourselves.

This time and energy could have gone elsewhere if we had just allowed ourselves to resist the escape for a few moments, hours, or perhaps even day by day. (See Chapter entitled "We Run, We Search".)

The other part of the story is the "ugly wallpaper" analogy which goes like this: by constantly finding escape mechanisms (avoiding) instead of living and facing life, even when it's scary or anxiety provoking, we create an "alternate life" or *"alternate little room" off of the main corridor of life.*

This alternate life is ultimately *very limited, small, and narrow, like a room with ugly wallpaper that we don't even like. What was once an escape, is now like a prison, which brings feelings of hopelessness and despair. Life just becomes a cruel series of never-ending attempts to seek the next "fix".*

By habitually escaping the "real" life that we have, with both its pain and its joy, we create this alternate "life" that can never be as vibrant, creative, joyful, or energized as real life; nor can it be as scary or painful as real life may be sometimes.

The problem is that our "little room" may not be as scary or painful as real life, but it can never be as wonderful either.

This little room, with its ugly wallpaper that you hate, becomes, after a while, very suffocating and loathsome and traps you inside.

This is when people truly become hopeless and tired of living—in other words, *when the escape itself has become their lives*, which in turn becomes horrible to them…even worse than real life originally was for them.

Examples of attempts to escape the "cobwebs" by entering the room with the "ugly wallpaper" include someone who finds himself addicted to drugs or alcohol over the years, or someone who has been having secret affairs for many years.

Ultimately, it would be no surprise that the escapes lead both of these people towards feeling no emotional intimacy or tranquility anywhere (room with ugly wallpaper.)

Or think of someone who uses thrill seeking, risky financial decisions, or gambling as escapes from the cobwebs.

Again, they will find themselves with a life that is being lived in that little room with the ugly wallpaper, full of the added cobwebs of hopelessness, loneliness, and despair, in addition to the original feelings which they were trying to escape in the first place.

chapter

4 "We Fail with the Heart, Not the Brain"

I once had a patient tell me that she put three of her children through college and that the smartest of the three was the only one to fail out. However, it was also with this particular child that the patient had the most emotional conflict.

Be aware: if there is deep-seated emotional conflict between a parent and one of his or her children, whether conscious or unconscious, that is the child who will be at the greatest risk for having difficulties in school and later in life, as in the above example.

In general, I believe that the greater the emotional stress, conflict, or "trauma" in a person's life, first in our relationships with our parents when we are growing up, and, later, with our spouses, etc., the more difficult it is for us to focus and concentrate on things.

The way I explain it is that when we are stressed, the emotional centers of the brain pull the resources away from the other parts of the brain that are in charge of clear thinking.

The patient above had an "over-identification" conflict with the child who later failed out of school (see Chapter entitled "Identification"), which made that relationship a strained one from the start. It was the emotional strain in the relationship with the parent which set the child up for later difficulties concentrating in school. The siblings were spared and probably had a completely different experience with the very same parent.

An analogy I often use with my patients, is this one: picture a deer getting shot at by a hunter. If the deer were to survive, just imagine the emotional trauma and turmoil it must've gone through while getting shot at.

Now, if you can imagine that the deer can talk and you were to ask it if it noticed what color the sky was while it was getting shot at, or whether the ground was covered with grass or leaves or dirt at the time, it would probably tell you that it didn't know.

In fact, how could the poor deer remember these things, or even think at all, if it was getting shot at? Attention deficit disorder? No, more likely explainable by the emotional trauma (of getting shot at) blocking the ability to think clearly and calmly and in an orderly fashion as well as remembering details.

Well, in life, and especially when we are little, many of the things we go through stress us emotionally. Believe it or not, children take on the brunt of adults' anxiety and anger, even if it's subtle. As this stress accumulates it becomes harder and harder for that child to participate fully in life with all of their intellectual and personal potential and harder to experience true joy because of the accumulation of emotional trauma or "emotional noise" that gets in the way of calm focus and deliberate living.

So, to clarify the "over-identification" example above, if one of my children reminds me of myself on some unconscious or conscious level, I will act towards them in a non-neutral, somewhat distorted fashion because I'm really recognizing myself in them and reacting to myself.

Let's say there are parts of me which I have disdain for, or which the adults in my childhood had disdain for. I will now mistreat my child in those same ways to complete the circle for myself. In other words, to "finish the unfinished business" of my own childhood at that child's expense. Put bluntly, I will exact revenge from my child for the way I was treated as a child. Why not? After all, they are smaller and weaker and more vulnerable than we are right? (Take a look at the "Identification" Chapter for examples.)

The more we do this to kids, and the more we've experienced this ourselves growing up, the more "emotional noise" we will have accumulated which will absolutely get in the way of living and performing at our highest potential both in our work and in our intimate relationships. (See the "Bicycle of Life" Chapter.) Ultimately, it gets in the way of learning who we truly are and it gets in the way of experiencing true joy.

chapter

5 "Anxiety and Impulse Control"

If there's one thing I would pass along to people if I absolutely had to choose just one thing it would be this: keeping track of our internal anxiety and what we do with it in terms of "action" are of utmost importance in life.

The act of not doing anything at all even though we are wanting to because of intense anxiety, fear, panic, anger, etc., is called Impulse Control.

Most people's lives could be improved considerably simply by improving the skill of Impulse Control. With my patients I sometimes call this "biting the tongue".

For example, if your child does or says something that makes you feel some strong anxiety inside yourself (and probably an unpleasant feeling such as fear or worry, etc.), the natural impulse is to immediately try to correct the situation, or "fix" something.

These are important moments because they are just the moments where our own strong emotion will most definitely get in the way of our ability to guide the child's exploration of the situation *for themselves*.

In this situation I would refer you back to the LVAC model (see Chapter entitled "LVAC") to help you help your child work through the experience *for themselves* and help clarify it for yourself as well. I will talk about this more in a minute.

But first, know that if we do not control our impulse to "do something" or "comment" immediately, we are in danger of undermining the development of the child's healthy anxiety with our own anxiety, thereby sabotaging an opportunity for their growth and passing on our own baggage to them instead.

Say, for example, that your child comes to you and says that they are feeling bullied in school by another child. Your very first emotion, if you allow yourself to feel it, might reflect how you actually felt as a child being bullied. You will therefore have a very strong reaction and will probably "react" or "comment" somehow rather than help them work this situation out in *their* life by using the LVAC technique.

If you automatically tell them, "Just ignore the bully", or "You've got to defend yourself", now you're essentially telling your child what you wish you could have or would have done yourself back then. It is based on your experience and emotional reactions, not theirs.

If they can't do it, you might lose your patience with them (really with yourself as a child in that same situation), thus adding to their feeling of humiliation and aloneness and abandonment.

It is really your own anxiety you are reacting to and you're now losing focus on the child's process of working the matter through for themselves and your opportunity to "LVAC" with them.

So, if, instead, you hear them out (Listen), support them no matter what (Validate), get them to tell you some details so you can learn (Ask), and *then* try to come up with a possible plan or plans (Comment), *now* you've given them a healthy start to a process which they will incorporate and use themselves *with themselves* as adults later on.

Keep in mind that often we run up against our own limits as parents when dealing with situations involving our children with which we *identify* strongly ourselves subconsciously (see Chapter entitled "Identification".) The goal here is to recognize you've come up against a limit in your own development and use the LVAC model to guide you towards growth for both your child and yourself.

Let's pretend for example that through the LVAC process you've come to the conclusion that part of what needs to be done is exactly what gives you anxiety: talking with the other child's parent about the bullying. Well, that taps into one of your own issues with confrontation and protecting yourself from bullies doesn't it? Now that it involves your child, you have an opportunity (and very strong motivation!) to do better for them AND to help yourself heal by doing what's necessary.

chapter

6

"A Child's Perspective"
(Automatic Pilot)

Picture yourself for a moment as a child. But not just any child. Picture yourself as a child having a hard time with a parent. Why you ask? Because this can help us understand our interactions with our own children better (or our nephews, nieces, grandkids, neighbors' kids, etc.)

Here I am. I'm a child having trouble with a parent.

Why does dad treat me so mean? When I'm hurt or afraid, why does he yell at me?

OR

Why does mom get so nervous and upset when I'm confused about my schoolwork or when I get hurt?

OR

Why do I feel so confused when dad hits me and I run over to mom who is the one who told on me in the first place?

OR

Why do I feel ashamed or stupid after mom scolds me?

OR

Why do the adults ignore me when all I want is a few minutes of *focused time* not just when they "have to" do something for me or fix something?

When we have children, or care for someone else's children we are placed in the unique position of having a vulnerable little human at our disposal.

This means that, if we were yelled at, humiliated, hit, or ignored as children, we will have the perfect opportunity to carry on that tradition with the next generation as well. Why not? After all, as I've said before, they are smaller and weaker than we are, and for the first few years of their lives they have to obey us no matter what we choose to do with them.

Well, here's the rub: we tend to act towards the next generation (usually our own kids) in similar ways and with the (often subconscious) intent of recreating our own childhood experiences but this time with ourselves in control and the child as our "target".

In effect, we switch into "Automatic Pilot", meaning we subconsciously give what we got when we were kids. Or we try so hard to do the opposite that we still hurt them.

For example: if my experience as a child was to have my mother become nervous when I wasn't sure what I was doing in school or of her being overly afraid of my getting hurt while playing, I'm likely to not be able to help my child modulate these situations very well.

Or, I may be so wary of repeating these things with my kids that I do just the opposite and am too relaxed or permissive with them and I don't give them the structure and guidance they need. It's still Automatic Pilot, only from the opposite direction: I'm still reacting to *my own* childhood experiences instead of truly addressing this particular child.

If, when I wanted to cry or was afraid, my father simply said I should "suck it up and be a man", then, of course, I won't have learned (experienced) first hand in my heart how to help a child who is feeling afraid or is crying. My Automatic Pilot when my kids are in this same situation will be to either act the same way he did OR just the opposite: again, neither is really a neutral or truly focused way of addressing my child's own situation. I'm simply still reacting to my father.

Now of course, these are generalizations I realize, but they do fit the stories of many many people who come to see me in my office.

The key part here is that it does not take much to improve this whole dynamic so we can avoid slipping into "Automatic Pilot" with our kids. The first step is to *recognize* it when it's happening.

So, if I'm recognizing that in certain situations I'm not as "even-keeled" or "adult-like" or "effective" with my children, OR if for some reason I can't get myself to be emotionally available (or available at all) to them, chances are I've just found one of these tricky spots from my own childhood with my own parents.

For example if I simply feel bored or too distracted to pay attention to my child in the evening after working all day (or at the end of the day with him), I'm probably not only tired, but hitting tricky territory from my own childhood. Chances are the adults around me did not focus on me the way I needed them too at these times, otherwise I would have learned what this felt like to receive firsthand (in my heart), and I'd have it to give instinctively.

A good trick is to watch another adult (spouse, etc.) without the same tricky spots handle these moments so you can see an alternative way of acting with the child in these situations.

For example, if it's difficult for you to focus on your child at certain times, observe how the other person does it and literally begin to *copy* them. If there are times when you feel overly angry or nervous with what your child does, try to observe (or recall) someone else's way of handling it if possible.

Different people have different tricky spots from their own childhoods, so what's difficult for you may not be for someone else and vice versa.

There's lots to learn from observing how others handle moments that are difficult for you.

chapter

7

"We Run, We Search: Looking for Structure"

Here's the scenario: you wake up on a Saturday or Sunday morning, or whatever day(s) off from work you may have, and have a feeling of free floating anxiety; just not sure what to do with yourself. Soon enough, you become even more uncomfortable, perhaps eventually to the point of feeling irritable or extremely out of sorts, maybe even a bit confused.

So what is this feeling? And what do people do when they're feeling it?

I once knew a man who would literally get migraine headaches when he had a vacation from work. All that unstructured time was quite unhealthy for him actually, as he would do all sorts of unhealthy things to try and feel better and less anxious, such as drinking too much, or becoming irritable with his wife and children. By the time the vacation was over, he was exhausted and felt guilty about how he'd spent the time.

Turns out, his work gave his life vital structure that he needed. Without it, he just didn't know how to manage himself or his environment very well, which led to unbearable anxiety for him.

Believe it or not, the feeling he experienced is the pain of anxiety caused by a lack of *"structure"*. When you have a day off, or perhaps don't have much structure in your daily life to begin with, this sort of anxiety often arises.

What's more, people usually do not recognize this anxiety for what it is, and instead move right ahead to trying to get rid of it, often in destructive ways (see Chapters entitled "Pain", and "Anxiety and Impulse Control".)

So what are some of these ways?

Well for example, being short or irritable with your loved ones (taking it out on them), or compulsively spending or shopping or viewing internet websites, or looking for physical intimacy (sex), or perhaps drinking, doing drugs, or gambling. Or even finding something to "keep yourself busy" such as more work.

As you can see, some of these ways of coping with the lack of structure are more obviously destructive, and some are more subtle. For example, one very subtle, destructive "solution" to this unbearable anxiety which some people find themselves employing is self-mutilation or cutting themselves: for them it adds structure and relieves the pain of intense anxiety.

All of which leads to this: if you really observe carefully, most people are either "running" or "searching" when they're not working or given some form of structure to cling to.

They're either searching for structure of some kind (as in the above list of examples), or they're running from the pain of their free-floating anxiety. It's really just a matter of degree for each person, in terms of how functional or dysfunctional their solution to the "problem" is.

In fact, the ever-present search for structure to calm ourselves can actually look like addictive behavior. Even though it may not involve drugs or alcohol, the idea is the same: we look for immediate ways of running from the anxiety pain, the pain of not having structure.

I believe that certain very structured professions lend themselves well to those of us who become anxious with lack of structure: medicine (including nursing), teaching, clergy, military, law enforcement, etc. These are fields in which a person can cling to the structure and hierarchy and avoid the confusion and anxiety of life, at least when they're at work.

These are also some of the main professions I treat in my practice. For what? Why, for anxiety of course (and its cousin, depression.)

It's not uncommon for a person, for example, to feel like two different people: the one who excels at their job, and the one who is at the "bottom of the class" at home (where there is less structure.)

In the end, what we are really looking for in all this, though we don't usually realize it consciously, is *connectivity*. It is simple: when we humans feel connected to others in a nurturing, empathetic way, the addictive behaviors (ie. the searching and running) go away naturally.

This might take the form of getting empathy or consideration from another person, or perhaps feeling their admiration or respect for you, or maybe just feeling like the apple of someone's eye.

Structure becomes less important, as we are soothed and satiated by this connectivity.

Look at children: if you give them a chunk of your completely focused time, they invariably become calmer and they themselves have less anxiety and can concentrate better.

Why? Because they're feeling *connected* to you. And best of all, you feel calmer because you are focusing on something too, something healthy: them! Everybody wins.

In fact, I'll often tell a patient who has children to experiment with literally timing themselves on their watch for fifteen minutes to completely focus on their kids, without allowing their minds to go elsewhere for that fifteen minutes; in other words to "lose themselves" (and their anxiety) in their children.

The activity itself doesn't matter: it might be bath time, play time, reading, homework, whatever.

The same goes with our adult relationships. Most people still crave this kind of focus and attention from others, such as from a spouse, but just don't realize it.

So, instead, they focus on and pour their energies into how to get rid of this annoying, vaguely indescribable pain they feel when they wake up on a free-form Saturday or Sunday morning feeling anxious, irritable, and a bit lost, instead of maybe sharing those feelings with a fellow adult and getting re-connected that day.

chapter

8

"Restraint"

If there is one skill you need to learn in adulthood, one skill that needs to be honed to near perfection, and one skill that can arguably contribute the most to more fulfilling, healthier relationships with both adults and children, it is Restraint.

If a husband comes home from work frustrated and tired and "needs" to unload his frustration, he may immediately start in on his wife or children, for example. This can be very subtle, or blatant.

Obviously, if he starts yelling at everyone, that is pretty blatant. But, what about if he just starts talking about his day calmly enough to whomever happens to be in his path? Well, the problem here is that he has not restrained himself enough to allow a few moments to assess the other person or people he is about to unload on.

What if, for example, his wife is also overwhelmed or frustrated or tired? Or what if the kids really need to be heard first and have been awaiting his arrival from work? Or what if his wife is upset about something and is waiting for an opportunity to speak with him and instead he starts unloading his own issues onto her? Can this not lead to anger, resentment, and ultimately *contempt?* (See Chapter entitled "Marriage Part I".)

What if the wife and husband are experiencing some difficulties with the children or with finances? Is it very adult like for one spouse to unload their own anxiety or anger about the situation onto the other?

You'd be surprised how many couples work this way: one spouse is upset by something and will not feel better until they've made the other spouse upset as well. I've seen instances where the person literally cannot feel relieved until the other person is upset; then they can walk away feeling that they've unloaded.

What they've also often done is helped build resentment and possibly contempt in the relationship for the short-term gain of dumping on the other person so they can feel better.

Would it not be better if we could hone the skill of Restraint in our lives, whether it's with our children, our spouses, our families of origin, or our friends and neighbors?

I am continually amazed in my daily life outside my office setting, by how little Restraint adults show. At the very least, people should practice the old adage of "counting to ten" before they say things to other people. And, more ideally, we should learn to "bite the tongue" and think about what we want to say to the people in our lives when we're upset or overwhelmed.

When we simply follow our instincts, we are acting as when we were children in our families of origin. We are simply acting any which way we please and *waiting for consequences or limits from the other person.* Instead, we should be setting those limits ourselves the best way we can, unlike when we were children.

In fact, I believe that *Restraint is one of the key skills adults can have or develop, which truly separates us from children.*

I suppose Impulse Control would be another good name for Restraint. Whatever we choose to call it, we adults need to use it in relating to our fellow adults, and to our children. Too often the way we hurt others, especially our children, and the way we breed contempt, is through poor impulse control.

We need to learn to hold on to our anxiety and not immediately seek to "discharge it" just long enough to consider the feelings of the person we are about to engage with, especially if that person is a child. (See Chapter entitled "Anxiety and Impulse Control".)

Children are very susceptible to adults' lack of Restraint in so many ways. And, of course, our difficulties with this skill become their difficulties with it when they grow up and have relationships and children of their own.

chapter

9

"The Trauma Gap"

This is a curious concept, which has been a major theme for my patients over the years: I call it the "trauma gap."

The trauma gap is the period of time between when something traumatic happens to you, (such as a verbal or physical boundary violation), and when you fully recognize and acknowledge it.

So, for example, if somebody is violating a boundary with you in some way, and you have a momentary feeling or impulse to fight it but you make this impulse go away instead of setting a limit right there and then; instead, allowing that person to keep doing what they're doing, that's an example of the trauma gap.

How about that neighbor who, in the midst of an innocent enough interaction, sort of invites himself or "dumps" his children onto you under the guise of a "play date", while he goes off to do something fun for himself? Or what about someone at work who has a way of making you feel bad or guilty or ashamed in front of your boss? How about when your sibling, or perhaps your spouse, takes on an angry or aggressive tone seemingly out of the blue? Or what if you're at the supermarket and someone is rude or intrudes upon your space?

These are examples which happen to us all the time. Yet we are often left in a state of "mini-shock" and paralyzed. Only later do we fully realize what we should have or could have done or said, only to be stuck now with feelings of inadequacy, self-loathing, or depression. Trauma gap.

What's needed here is to begin to allow ourselves to recognize when boundaries are being broken, no matter how subtle. The first step is merely to *recognize when it's happening*, not to necessarily do anything about it.

You'd be surprised at how hard this first step really is. Yet, it's the key step in "closing the trauma gap", ie., in becoming more "in step" or "in sync" with boundary violations as they are occurring to you or your loved ones.

The ultimate goal is greater self-control and greater personal power and options in interpersonal communication.

No one says you have to correct or set limits every time; but simply honing the skill of recognizing and acknowledging to yourself when a boundary is being violated will make you feel better about yourself and feel more in control and give you more options.

Once you get good at the *recognition step*, you will be prepared to tap into and practice a wide variety of creative, compassionate, and empathetic ways to set limits so that you can enjoy your interpersonal relationships to the fullest.

Remember, good, healthy boundaries help us *keep* relationships, whereas poor boundaries often destroy them.

chapter

10

"Pain and the 'Spot on the Page' Analogy"

We humans are always attempting to distract ourselves from emotional pain. Whether by drugs or alcohol, by sexual pleasures (affairs, etc.), by thrill seeking or adrenaline rushes, or by "workaholism" or personal chaos, I would guess that we use a good portion of our energies working out ways to avoid feeling unpleasant emotions such as anxiety or loneliness in our lives.

The problem with this way of living is that it creates less and less focus on *living* and more and more focus on the distractions from life's pain. No wonder that eventually depressive- or anxiety-type feelings become overwhelming and a person begins to lose the sense of *who they really are*-- meaning what they like, do not like, desire, do not desire, etc.-- and they continue to feel "stuck."

In my work with people I often use the "Spot on the Page" analogy, which goes like this: emotional discomfort (anxiety, fear, sadness, loneliness, etc.) can be compared to a big black spot on a piece of paper. One of the goals of adult life is not so much to make the spot disappear (which is what people want), but to grow our ability to bear these emotions for longer periods of time.

In the analogy, it's not that the spot gets smaller, but the *page gets bigger.* In other words, our lives become broader and more robust, and the pain that we could not bear, beginning in childhood, we now learn to begin to bear as adults. Since adults generally have more brute strength and resources than children, if we think about it for a moment, we as adults can often bear things that we had no chance with as children.

There is incredible personal power in this; I have seen it over and over again in many different people. *Once their ability to hold on to the moment grows, whether that be loaded with loneliness, sadness, fear, anxiety, or whatever else, they "break through" to the other side and no longer need to do anything to distract themselves (such as drink, shop, eat, have sex, drive recklessly, etc.)*

In fact, once we learn to not distract ourselves so much, we have a chance to feel a bit lighter, clearer, and less distracted and confused about what we want and who we are. One might say that the "cobwebs" begin to clear and living becomes a more elegant, simpler process, complete with pain when it comes, which we can now begin to bear without self-destructive or distracting behaviors. (See Chapter entitled "Cobwebs and Ugly Wallpaper".)

Simply put: distraction equals creating *more* "cobwebs" whereas working to bear emotional pain clears them. The cobwebs lead to more depression, guilt, anxiety, confusion, etc., not a real, permanent solution to these things.

chapter

11

"Marriage Part One"

One of the most common things people come to see me about is trouble in their marriages or with their significant others.

A long time ago, while shopping for wedding rings, I once read a description of what a wedding ring stands for. It went something like this: "The ring stands for…seamless unity without beginning or end…the ties of friendship, trust, faith, and love." It went on to explain that the ring is supposedly worn on the *left* ring finger in order to be as close as possible to the heart.

Well, what happens then, to all these couples who experience problems in their marriages? Why the affairs? Why the comments of "we're like roommates or work partners"? Why the resentments, anger, or even rage and contempt? Why the tremendous disappointments? Why the eventual stoppage of all physical intimacy and the consequences which may follow as well as the causes of it to begin with (see also the Chapter entitled "For Men")?

The fact is that, unlike a new relationship or family of origin relationships (eg. mom, dad, siblings), a marriage is a *unique relationship*; one in which we must learn a *brand new way of behaving and interacting with another person.*

We really can't act towards our spouses the same way we'd act with our "family". (Although a spouse becomes, in a sense, our family, it's still different). Most people really do eventually just act towards their spouses the way they are used to acting and reacting in their lives starting with childhood and their families of origin. This is where the problems begin.

Let's look at some key words regarding marriage: Trust, Disappointment, Empathy, Support, Consideration, and Tone.

Notice how I've left out the word love. The reason is that in my work with people, it becomes difficult to pin down what they mean by the word "love", but it is never a question what they mean by Trust, Disappointment, Empathy, Support, Consideration, and Tone.

First, let's look at Tone. And let's expand the definition of Tone to not only mean literally the tone of our voice, but also the *intent* and *effect* of what we are saying to the other person.

If we're dealing with our families of origin, we're usually not aware of the tone of our voice. It's the same tone we've developed as children and brought along with us and refined into adulthood. Perhaps it's flavored by the yelling, the sarcasm, the disdain, the humiliating and shaming, the intimidating, the guilt laying, the ultimatums, the closed-ended statements, etc., that we were raised with.

In other words, we just "let it fly" (emotion) the way it feels when it's coming up to our mouths from the heart and gut without any truly "adult" editing or consideration.

This is NOT a good idea in a marriage. Remember, a marriage is a *unique* relationship. *These ways of speaking to our spouses place both ourselves and our spouses back into childhood with our families of origin.* What's the problem with that?

Well, for one thing, we generally do not have physical intimacy (ie. sex) with our families of origin, so when someone tells me that they are no longer desirous physically of their spouse, or that they've had an affair, this issue eventually comes up. They've subconsciously placed both themselves and their spouse back into the family of origin and the marriage is no longer a unique, adult relationship, but more of an endless continuation of their childhood.

Furthermore, improper Tone and lack of Consideration of marriage as a unique, adult relationship eventually leads to Disappointments and breaks in Trust.

The only path I know to getting back the Trust is through *Empathy and Support*.

Yes, we're supposed to be aware of our Tone with our spouses. We're supposed to actually "behave" ourselves with them deliberately, in order to avoid slipping back into a childhood stance and having them do the same.

I'm continuously amazed by the lack of Empathy and Support which spouses offer each other just because they are unaware of all of this. *They interact with each other by instinct and reflexes that were developed in childhood with their parents and siblings.*

Marriage requires the development of a brand new balance of reactions and deliberate attempts to interact in a new way that we've never had to do before.

Past Disappointments do have an effect on today's Trust. Whenever I am able to witness the interactions of a couple together in my office, or anywhere for that matter, I am acutely aware of any resentment and anger in one or both person's voices. When I gently point this out, it eventually leads to discussion of past Disappointments, including even those from yesterday or earlier that day.

When we begin to no longer have faith in the other person's ability or good, supportive intentions towards us, we naturally begin to have less Trust in them. This even further triggers those childhood reactions within us from all the Disappointments from the way we were treated back then by parents, siblings, or whoever.

So, of course, we are driven further apart from our spouse, not closer together, as they now get not only our current resentments but they also inherit those from our past as well.

It is really only through Empathy and Support for one another that these things can be avoided and even healed, within a healthy marriage. A good tool for offering each other Empathy and Support is by using the LVAC model of communication (see Chapter entitled "LVAC".)

As we see, Marriage is also a *unique* relationship because it can allow a rare chance for each spouse to heal from childhood disappointments, humiliations, abuses, etc. But this is not the automatic result in most marriages. (See Chapter entitled "Marriage Part Two".)

In fact, experience shows that, unless we deliberately work on the marital relationship in the ways described above, the default result in a marriage is the opposite one; in other words the re-traumatization of the spouses by each other and the continuation of childhood for each of them as they throw themselves and each other back into the patterns of their families of origin. Destructive, not healing.

chapter

12

"For Men"

Three major points stand out in my practice over and over again with respect to men.

The first, is that *men and women are "wired differently" with regards to sex*. Now, you won't find any scientific papers to back this up; this is purely from my clinical experience with men, women, and couples.

For most of the women I speak with, there is generally a need first for feeling emotionally intimate before any physical intimacy is really possible or desired. On the other hand, for the majority of the men that I speak with, there is a feeling of emotional closeness once there is physical intimacy.

Now, of course, there are exceptions to this observation.

However, the above guideline remains the case for many of the couples I've treated: often, the woman in the relationship comes in feeling that the man is "distant" or "selfish" or "self absorbed" or "not interested in me", which ultimately leads to less and less desire for physical intimacy which the man then complains about.

This becomes quite a "Catch-22" situation, as the man becomes more and more resentful about the lack of physical intimacy, which leads to even less emotional consideration, tenderness, and support towards the woman.

What's needed here is a two-prong approach. On the one hand, the couple must begin to work on building back the emotional intimacy first, above all else. (See Chapter entitled "Marriage Part One".)

Then, believe it or not, I'll often also suggest to them that they set aside some time one evening a week if possible to also allow for some form of physical intimacy (not necessarily intercourse, by the way.)

This sets up the stage (I've seen it over and over!) wherein the man begins to have more tender feelings towards the woman, and his tendency towards pressuring her for sex or acting obnoxiously or selfishly all the time decreases. What happens then is that he'll often tend to be more attentive (less resentment towards her for no sex) and considerate, and he'll also tend to work harder on rebuilding the emotional connection with her. **Wiring difference!**

The second big theme I see is that men often forget that the way they act towards their daughters may very well (and often does) influence who and how their daughter will date and even their selection of a spouse.

For example, if the father is domineering and self-centered, and hardly ever has time or focus for his daughter, guess what? He shouldn't be surprised when his daughter brings home a "real prize" for him to meet one day as his future son-in-law. (By the way, mothers too can influence this dynamic and are not off the hook either.)

Most fathers I treat really do begin to understand the impact of their behaviors once this dynamic is made clear. Every dad I've ever met has had at the very least enough guilt to want to change once they think about how they can influence their daughter's future, including her safety emotionally and even physically. They begin to act more tenderly and gently with more direct attention and consideration.

The third theme I've noticed in my work is that men tend to "stay up late", after their wives and children are asleep for the night. This is often done under the guise of wanting to "stay up to read" or "watch the game" or "the show".

What I see is that this practice often eventually leads to decreased emotional intimacy with the wife and family. It often represents or reinforces a sense of youthful freedom and an *unfinished transition to a committed married life with a family.* The chance for true, adult intimacy and peace is unlikely in this scenario and problems often arise eventually.

For example, men can often get themselves into trouble during these "late nights". Some examples I've encountered are late-night internet addictions, spending money, affairs, drinking, and gambling to name a few.

Again, this is a generalization of course, but on the other hand my experience with people tells me over and over again that this is more often true than not. I'll often suggest to a couple whose relationship is in trouble that they start by making sure that they go to bed *together* at night. For some men, this is harder than you might think, and can often lead to some fruitful exploration as to why it is so difficult for them.

chapter

13 "The Communication Engine"

Interestingly enough, communicating our needs is often one of the major hurdles we humans experience; thus the idea of the "Communication Engine". I'll explain this idea in a minute, but first, a bit about difficult communication.

We are often inhibited by fear, anxiety, guilt, shame, and any number of other strong feelings, either conscious or sub-conscious; all set in motion by our earlier experiences as children, when we were powerless and lacked experience.

We either overreact, or "under-react", or perhaps avoid entirely. Perhaps we grow so uncomfortable we avoid certain people or places or jobs or activities.

Now here's the thing:

As I tell my patients, *I truly believe that we adults can always find a way to communicate what we need to*

say, in a compassionate, heartfelt way, no matter what.
The major challenge is finding the right way for each
situation, a skill which, for most of us, can be improved
greatly and even mastered with time.

In fact, a major difference between adults and
children is that we adults have the advantages of 1)
experience and creativity, 2) resourcefulness, and 3)
stamina, far beyond what children have available to them
to hone communication skills.

The problem is that many, if not most, adults fall
back into childhood patterns when they are in situations
requiring difficult communication. For example, we can
feel trapped or stuck, without options or embarrassed, or
even afraid or paralyzed.

So then, a major skill of adulthood is the mastery of
communication.

As I tell my patients, I'm not so much interested in
how "direct" or "passive" a communication option is,
especially when first building these skills. I'm more
interested in whether or not *the person feels better once*
they've communicated their truth in the best way they can
to the other person.

For example, if a coworker is pretty obnoxious to
you, or somehow undermines your sense of self-
confidence or peace at work, you have many options

regarding how to communicate your displeasure with that person.

These options run the gamut from direct confrontation, (compassionately, of course), to simply making a decision inside yourself to not allow that person past certain boundaries by using gentle feedback or withdrawal of your attention as communications. Often, we have more power than we think by simply staying silent or removing ourselves from someone's presence if they make us feel uncomfortable. Again, depending on the level of skill development, it's not so important how "direct" or "passive" a technique may be; what matters is that you feel better once you communicate and are no longer hold it in.

Again, the options are many, and I truly believe that a thoughtful approach to these communications, using our experience, creativity, resourcefulness, and stamina, is empowering, regardless of the specific techniques used.

A patient once observed that she became very "tired" when faced with such challenges. This "tiredness" is a good example of "psychological tiredness" rather than "physical tiredness". In other words, she was getting tired because such attempts at expressing herself were new to her; new skills with lots of fear and anxiety in the way of them, making her feel an inner resistance or "tiredness".

This is where the idea of the "Communication Engine" comes in. When we're first learning to use our adult advantages to communicate our needs, we are required to muster up *extra energy* to build these skills. So many of my patients will say to me, "Well, that's great doctor, but doing this stuff is very draining for me."

Well, because it *is* draining at first, I like to picture, in every person, a shiny new engine which most of us never used much in childhood, since kids don't have as much power and as many options as we adults do.

We must realize that it is going to take extra energy at first to practice these new communication skills and to get to know ourselves as adults who can handle things in more competent and complete ways than children can. It is the "Communication Engine" which will give us this energy once we learn to tap into it.

It is a strange thing for most people to imagine that, though they feel tired or overwhelmed, they can actually push themselves further as long as there is the focus of skill building in mind.

In this case, as we learn to use our experience, creativity, resourcefulness, and stamina to communicate our needs to others, we learn to tap into the stores of energy we each have which is designed for just that purpose. Yes it takes energy, but it won't kill you, and actually, you'll get used to it and expand your abilities and options in life. It's only new because you weren't given a chance to develop it in childhood.

And once you start getting used to having your internal needs heard and respected in the world (what I call "winning"), and to a good extent met, it is very hard to think about going back to the more childlike ways from whence most of us came, even if they do require "less energy".

chapter

14 "The 'Am I OK?' Question vs. the 'How am I doing?' Question"

There is a fundamental difference between needing to know from someone whether you are "OK" versus wanting their feedback as to how you are doing.

This may sound obvious but is it?

How many of you look to your jobs, or more specifically, to your boss or other influential people at work, for signs that you are "OK" rather than specific professional feedback regarding how you are doing?

The first question is much more personal, and it is really not the privilege of people at work to determine whether or not you are fundamentally "OK". Instead, this question is first asked and answered in childhood by one's caregivers, usually the parents, and later on we look for signs from our spouses and other close family and friends.

But some people are hurt over and over again because they are searching for confirmation or validation from the wrong sources.

Sticking to the work example, if several people at work get a pay raise and you do not, how deeply would this affect you? Would it cause you to feel "not OK" at a fundamental level and cause weeks or months of self-doubt and anxiety or even depression?

Or would you instead mentally categorize it as a "how am I doing" indicator, taking it less personally?

If an acquaintance or co-worker is mean to you, how deeply and personally do you feel this? Does it get past the superficial and send you spiraling into self-doubt, anxiety, or even self-blame and confusion about what you must have done wrong? Or do you try not to take it too personally, allowing yourself to either pursue clarification with them regarding what they said to you, or perhaps choosing not to address it immediately or to ignore it?

We must remember to mentally categorize the source of whatever feedback or comments we receive every day about ourselves in our lives. As they say, you must consider the source.

It is important to keep the very personal question of "am I OK" limited to the very closest people in our lives, starting with ourselves. For it is impossible to truly replace the original caregivers, parents, etc., with a source that will make us feel "OK" and viable in our lives. We certainly shouldn't look to just anybody for the answer to this question, but that's exactly what so many of us do in our daily lives by how we interpret or let affect us the things others say, or by how we read into issues at work.

That feeling of being "OK" ultimately has to come from our own sense of peace and acceptance of ourselves, and it helps to be surrounded by a few close friends and family that can help validate it for us.

Do not fall into the mistake of asking the "am I OK" question of people or institutions (eg. workplace, other organizations, etc.) that are in no position whatsoever to answer such a personal question without hurting you. For most situations, work included, the question should more accurately be, "How am I doing"; much less personal and not as potentially hurtful.

chapter

15 "Identification"

By the word "Identification" I mean specifically when we psychologically and often subconsciously identify with our children, and not in a healthy way either. Let me explain.

If one of my children reminds me of myself in some way, (ie. they look like me or act like me, or, heaven forbid, I've named them after myself or they have similar shortcomings as I do), then I've got a setup for an unhealthy identification with that child (see Chapters entitled "Anxiety and Impulse Control" and "Automatic Pilot".)

It is with that child that I will automatically and subconsciously have a more difficult time with, almost guaranteed.

When that child is having difficult times in life or is behaving poorly, I will be especially "triggered" because I have a subconscious identification with that particular kid.

For example, if they are humiliated or hurt, I will have a hard time acting towards them in an adult, helpful (see "LVAC" Chapter) manner, and instead I will *re-act* based on my own internal conflicts with myself and my own past experiences with this same issue.

This is the child to whom I will transfer all of my "baggage" from my own childhood and bump heads with the most. This is the child my patients inevitably describe as causing in them the strongest emotional reactions (often they describe feelings of "guilt", "frustration", or "confusion" when talking about this particular child.)

Well, there is no simple way around this problem except this: we must begin to "neutralize" or "clean up" our own internal reactions to this child before dealing with them, so that we can treat them just like the other kids, which I'll explain in a moment.

So, in other words, if you look at your daughter and automatically feel differently (more short tempered, confused, vulnerable, angry, etc.) than with your son or other daughter, well, you've very likely come up against an identification problem with that kid.

It is with this child that you'll need to examine your internal reactions before acting on them, which often requires the technique of "checking in" with a more neutral third party such as a spouse or therapist. This will go a long way towards "neutralization" of your own internal biased reactions towards this child. You will learn a lot about your own limits and childhood problems, which were never addressed.

Of course, the first step here is allowing yourself to believe that there is an issue inside of you regarding this particular child, and not allowing yourself to ignore this fact just because it is uncomfortable to think about or you feel guilty about your feelings.

Besides our own children, other people in our lives can uniquely "push our buttons" in other ways, and the process of dealing with this issue is similar to the process just discussed of neutralizing our reactions and identifications with our children before acting on them. This however, is for another chapter.

chapter
16   **"The Stuff of Life"**

When a patient tells me that they're feeling very anxious, or upset somehow and they don't know what to do with themselves or how to feel better, I'll often ask them *what it is they've been doing* during that time.

For example, one person told me that he felt awful one weekend and had no idea why or what to do about it. He barely could get himself out of bed and showered and dressed, and then he spent most of the day watching television, but not really able to relax enough to enjoy even that.

He did not take care of some of the things around the house that he had wanted to take care of; nor did he do some of the things he had planned to do for his pets and his car. And as for himself, he almost forgot to eat that day, and when he did, he was so hungry he gorged on fast food, which he had no intention of doing heading into the weekend.

Come Monday, he had a looming sense of failure and guilt, and, of course, anxiety.

What this person missed that weekend was *the stuff of life.*

All of those things that he knew he should do for himself, his home, his pets, and even his car, all went undone. Of course, one's subconscious mind keeps track of all of these "letdowns" in self-care and business that doesn't get done, and the person then becomes anxious, and, eventually, depressed or sad.

Remember that movie some twenty years ago, "Karate Kid", I believe it was called, where the boy wants to learn the magical secrets of the martial arts? He seeks out the wise guidance of a master martial artist whose first instructions to the boy were that he must wash the teacher's car and paint his fence. Now what's that got to do with mastering the magical martial arts skills, wonders the boy?

Well, much as in art, real life also dictates that we must "wash the car and paint the fence" in order to tend to ourselves and our lives properly. *This is the stuff of life.*

For there is no "magic" in feeling at peace with unstructured time (see Chapter entitled "We Run, We

Search".) If you have children, tend to them with focused care and attention. If you have pets, do the same. Tend to your spouse, your home, your basic car care. And, of course, tend to yourself. Take care of your health, both mental and physical, as they really are connected to one another. Make appointments with your primary care doctor and any specialists to help you keep an objective eye on yourself.

If we do not tend to the stuff of life, we can spend many years with a vague sense of anxiety and even depression and a negative sense of self, as we continuously search for the "magic" solution to make us feel better (see "Cobwebs and Ugly Wallpaper".)

chapter

17

"Raising Victims"

If you were to ask your neighbor if they would like their children to be somebody else's victims when they grow up, they'd most certainly say, "no way!"

Yet, observe how they behave with their children and you may find that their actions say otherwise, even if they're subtle.

For example, how about a father who is very inconsistently present for his daughter? Or puts her down, makes fun of or takes lightly her feelings, or hits her? Well, why would he be surprised if she eventually introduces him to her chosen spouse, who is a controlling and abusive (emotionally or physically or both) person?

Or a father who ignores his daughter or who is only there when it suits *him*? Or one who becomes more like a drug for his children than an example of a healthy, balanced relationship? For example, he treats them badly in general or somewhat ignores them, but then says or does the right things to apologize and win them over again, only to repeat the cycle over and over. Later on, drugs, alcohol, or various other escapes (see "Cobwebs and Ugly Wallpaper" and "We Run, We Search") become a way for the child to continue this pattern for themselves.

What about a mother who insists on knowing every little detail about her son's life to an intrusive level, including any and all sexual explorations both with himself and anyone else? What if she is easily offended by his attempts to set limits with her and she becomes angry with him or cold and withdrawing?

Or what if she (or the father) make fun of his tender feelings of fear or anxiety with such lines as "come on, don't be a wimp", or "buck up", or "be a man".

Why should anyone be surprised to later on discover that this same boy has trouble becoming emotionally intimate with women, or perhaps that he leads a double life or maybe keeps secrets from his spouse either sexually or otherwise. Or if he feels very lonely, despite being married and having children, as he subconsciously concludes that his emotions and real desires would be as misunderstood by or unacceptable to his spouse as they once were to his mother or father, thus keeping himself emotionally isolated or unavailable.

In fact, how about raising victims to lives of drug and alcohol dependence? How better to fill the emotional voids we can help create in our children by lack of focused, empathetic engagement than by these means of escapism? (See Chapters entitled "We Run, We Search" and "Cobwebs and Ugly Wallpaper".)

If a person feels alone and empty and unable to express themselves or their needs, or have their limits respected by others, they often turn to addictive behaviors to either numb themselves or provide temporary relief or pleasure. This can include drugs and alcohol, as well as sex, thrill seeking and risk taking, and, of course, perhaps the most subtle of them all, work and "keeping busy".

If we act out our frustration, anxiety, or other emotions (yes, including envy), towards our children without restraint (see Chapter entitled "Restraint"), we can bet that they will become victims, and, at times, perpetrators, depending on the situation, of somebody or something else later in life.

Over and over again I meet people who have routinely been taken advantage of by other people. Whether it be at their place of work, by their neighbors, by colleagues, or by family members; in large part because of earlier life experiences of being taken advantage of by the adults around them who had no restraint. These were adults who were subconsciously acting out their own childhood revenge upon their own children (see Chapters entitled "Restraint" and "Identification".)

We can best avoid raising victims if we approach our children with the LVAC technique described in the Chapter entitled "LVAC". This involves respecting who they are, not who we want them to be, as well as what *they* are feeling, not what we want them to feel or what *we* happen to be feeling at the moment. It also involves setting limits without being inappropriately punitive or shaming, or "blowing them out of the water" with overreactions.

chapter

18   "Emotional Stumps"

Have you ever met an emotional stump?

Most of us have. Or perhaps, like many of us, you
yourself have been one for at least part of your life, or you
may be married to one, or come from a family of "emotional
stumps".

*An emotional stump is a person who really hasn't
found either wheel of the bicycle of life yet.* Remember
from Chapter 2 ("The Bicycle of Life") that the two major
opportunities we have to learn the most about ourselves
are the work and love wheels of the bicycle of life.

Well, an important thing happens when a child is not
given the opportunity to experience the "LVAC" technique
very much in their lives (ie. "L"isten, "V"alidate, "A"sk, and
"C"omment --see Chapter 1 for a refresher.) That is, *they
miss an early opportunity to define themselves emotionally
both to themselves and to others.*

They eventually grow into adults who have a difficult time figuring out *what they really want or don't want, what they like or don't like.* In other words, they have not yet identified their *true inner selves.* (Remember from before that, in my estimation, an everyday definition of the true inner self is simply *what a person wants, doesn't want, likes, and doesn't like*—that's it.)

Thankfully, the work and love wheels of the bicycle are the second chance opportunities to overcome the lack of LVAC from our childhoods and find again the roots of our true inner selves even in adulthood.

In other words, finding what we want to do and who we want to be with are the ways we define our true selves.

Unfortunately, many, if not most people, do not really come to know this, and, for the most part, squander or are completely unaware of these opportunities.

How do they squander them or remain unaware?

Ask someone who has spent the last 40 years working at a particular job or career what they think about their work.

If the answer is something like, "It was okay, I guess…paid the bills…got lots of time off…good benefits….", etc., chances are they squandered one of the two major opportunities to really ignite their true inner selves (ie. the work wheel.)

Or, ask someone who's been married for 40 years about their marriage or their spouse.

If the answer is something like, "Well the devil you know is better than the one you don't", or, "I tolerated her", or "We are mostly like roommates", or, "I'm not sure I ever really loved him", etc., chances are they have missed the other major opportunity to tap into the power of their true inner selves (ie. love wheel.)

What does this mean?

Well, in our adult relationships, just as with children, we should be using LVAC and other empathy-driven communications to increase emotional intimacy. This way, a marital-type relationship is a real chance at mutual healing from the accumulated emotional traumas of each other's childhoods. Intimacy like this energizes and fuels us.

In fact, tapping into what we really desire in both the work and love wheels of life, produces joy and energy, curiosity and interest, rather than apathy, anxiety, sadness and lethargy.

Regarding work, when we've found something we are supposed to be doing (vocation or avocation) it also energizes and fuels us; it *sustains us*.

The energy and the joy we gain from working on the love and work wheels give our lives momentum, structure, and a pace of living, and they help us live our lives to the fullest.

Now, remember, the "emotional stump" has not done any of this, often through no real conscious or deliberate fault of their own. But the fact is, they have not yet really found what they like, don't like, want, and don't want in life; ie. they haven't found their true inner selves.

They can even appear to be successful and happy, but yet carry with them feelings of emptiness, loss, sadness, or free floating anxiety, *starting from their childhoods without much LVAC and continuing into their adulthoods without much refinement of the work and love wheels.*

They are usually most comfortable with a fairly limited routine in life, both in work and in their relationships; one that does not require much creativity, flexibility, risk, variety, or regular adaptation.

They tend to not nurture close relationships, and are not particularly energized or creative with regards to their work or hobbies.

They also will likely need to use various forms of escapism (see Chapters entitled "We Run, We Search" and "Cobwebs and Ugly Wallpaper"), and other ways to deal with the misalignment of their lives with their true inner selves. These are the ways in which they can at least feel temporary relief from and short-term happiness in their lives.

In effect, they are like tree stumps, with none of the beautifully developed branches and foliage of a fully nurtured tree in all of its awesome beauty and strength.

The roots are there, but nobody has helped them harness the power of *who* they really are. In other words, the sense of what they really truly *would like, don't like, want, or don't want.*

Look around you: unfortunately there really are many more stumps than trees.

chapter

19   **"Marriage Part Two"**

The purpose of this little chapter is quite simple.

Quite regularly, both in my office and outside, I find myself expressing my opinion to others as to why we choose the spouses that we choose.

I have come to this opinion through years of seeing first hand and almost without exception, (unless two people are "arranged" to marry by tradition or other circumstances beyond their free choice of a spouse), the kinds of troubles people encounter in their marriages and where these troubles originate.

Keeping in mind that this concept can sound quite strange and perhaps even implausible at first, I'll attempt to share it with you anyway, since it proves itself true, to some degree or other, over and over again in my work with people.

In short, I find that people choose their spouses partly *consciously* (physical attraction, admiration and respect for accomplishments, convenience, similar interests, "good family", etc.) and partly *subconsciously*.

As you might guess, the stuff I'm going to try to explain occurs mostly in the subconscious part, since, by definition, the conscious part you already know about.

It is my opinion and observation that, other than the conscious factors listed above, people choose each other subconsciously by how well they "yolk" with each other in the subconscious part of themselves.

Let me explain.

For example, if two people are out on a date and one makes all the decisions and takes the lead, perhaps this may *feel right* (think, *subconscious*) to the other person and they might come away with a good overall feeling about their date.

Perhaps for someone else, this may be uncomfortable, making them feel as though their date is too controlling or suffocating.

What makes one person appreciate and feel comfortable with all the decisions being made for them, and the other feel put off by it?

Well, it seems that it has everything to do with the differences in each individual's background, both genetically (ie. their inborn "temperment" or "nature"), as well as experientially (ie. what they were exposed to growing up, meaning "environmental" or "nurture".)

The importance of this is that, regardless of comfort or discomfort with the date's approach, it is almost always the case that the person does not know consciously, in words, the full extent to which something is either turning them off of or onto their date.

But they will have a *feeling or hunch*, and instead of really knowing consciously what's going on, they're more likely to either 1) go out on a second date, or 2) not, based on this feeling.

Because they're not fully aware of what is being triggered to either make them comfortable or uncomfortable with the other person, we know that they're also not really understanding themselves either, which leads to problems down the line with their choices as relationships develop and full personalities become evident.

For example, if the person who is comfortable with all the decisions being made for them ultimately begins (say, years later) to feel somewhat annoyed, or resentful towards their spouse, they likely will not know why consciously. In fact, they are confused about how something that originally attracted them to their spouse, now repulses them.

It's just that what made them feel "comfortable" initially, was actually based on their own subconscious, unknown stuff, which they don't really understand about themselves to begin with.

In other words, I often won't fully know consciously why I like or dislike someone else, meaning that chances are I'm also reacting to them from my own unprocessed, unknown, and unfinished internal conflicts (ie. the subconscious.)

For example, perhaps my mother or father (or whoever the primary caretaker was) did not allow for much self-exploration or self-determination for their children. Low and behold, later on in life, when a potential spouse "takes control", I might feel "comfortable" with this at first, even though it's not necessarily healthy for me.

Eventually, I'll experience an internal "rebellion" against this control, and it'll come in the form of resentment or annoyance at my spouse. Trouble is, it's not completely their fault either, since my own unfinished, unconscious "business" from childhood yolked well with theirs. Now, I'm not only angry with them, but super-angry because they're also going to inherit the original, repressed (subconscious) anger towards my parents from childhood as well for doing the same thing! Now that's a lot of potential anger and destruction in the marriage.

This is one of the main aspects of the work I do with people who are having trouble in their relationships. The first step is helping them see how they initially "yolked" with their spouse and thus chose each other to begin with. The next step is helping each of them work through those initial, unfinished conflicts within themselves from childhood, which made them feel comfortable with each other at first and that later caused problems

Along the way people also often realize that neither spouse is really fully "right" or "wrong"; that they've really both been reacting towards each other based on unfinished, unprocessed childhood issues with their respective parents, siblings, or whomever.

The beauty of this is that a marital type relationship forces us to find these subconscious "buttons" *within ourselves*, since we yolked or fit in so well with each other initially based on them.

The next step, however, is to follow through and use this insight to help each other heal from the unfinished childhood business, which is what the therapy is supposed to help do. *In doing so, the spouses also heal themselves as individuals as well.*

To repeat this last, very important bit: *working towards a healthier marriage requires, per force, that each individual begin to heal within themselves.* This means that a very elegant "side effect" of the whole process of finding your spouse, then having those same factors drive you apart, followed by working these issue through, is the *healing of the self.*

Unfortunately, what often happens instead is that people either spend so many years resenting each other that contempt sets in (see Chapter entitled "Marriage Part One"), or that one or both spouses "act out" in destructive ways to deal with the marital disconnect, thus further driving themselves apart from one another (see the next Chapter.)

chapter

20 "The Deliberate Life"

Whenever I'm talking with one of my patients, or anyone really, I'm always interested in how much of their day to day life seems to be "deliberate" versus being dictated by various reactions both internally and externally.

For example, let's say a man is feeling disconnected from his spouse or significant other. That they are more like "roommates" than anything.

Let's also say that he's feeling lots of stress (good or bad) at work, or in other areas of his life. He's also got various pressures and responsibilities, which feel overwhelming to him at times.

Well, in my experience with people, this man has the risk factors required for some form of "non-deliberate" life choices.

For example, he may "decide" to have an affair, or he may use drugs or alcohol to momentarily escape the pressure, or perhaps he may begin to show up late to work or procrastinate. His boundaries with others may slowly loosen up in various destructive or self-sabotaging ways, or he may make one or more purchases to temporarily make himself feel better.

In other words, because he is actually feeling disconnected from the most intimate people in his life (spouse or significant other, children, etc.), he is at risk for what some call "acting out behaviors".

The point here is that these "choices" are often more accurately described as *reactions* to internal or external pressures than they are well thought-out, deliberate choices or adult decisions.

We know this because these are the very choices which most of the time prove to be damaging to the person's life, whether it be to their relationships, their finances, their physical or emotional health, etc. Ultimately, it is NOT what the person really wants.

So why do we humans do this?

Because we are feeling disconnected, anxious, lost, empty, bored, etc., you name it.

So what should we be doing about it?

What needs to be done is a "gear switch" back to "deliberate living".

In other words, we need to get back into our *real* lives, with our *real* emotions, and our *real* relationships.

How?

To start, you are better off taking a walk or throwing yourself into serving your children or other dependents, or perhaps doing something healthy for yourself such as preparing a healthy meal, or tackling a task you've been putting off, than taking the "reactive" options listed above (see Chapter entitled, "We Run, We Search".)

If you're feeling out of sorts, or have free floating anxiety, why not sit down with a pen and paper and list the things that are bothering or worrying you?

Maybe you've been procrastinating something important (or lots of things), or maybe you're worried about your physical health and have not followed through with seeing your doctor about it.

Whatever it is, you're better off listing it out and discussing with someone why you are putting it off, or what your feelings are about it, than ignoring it completely. Whenever we put something off for a long time it takes on a power and an insurmountability far beyond the actual issue at hand. This is not healthy, not emotionally, and not physically.

You might be surprised how freeing it is, and how healing, to begin to make your decisions in your day to day life *deliberately*, and not *reactively* or based on subconscious fears or conflicts.

Some other examples of deliberate living to take with you:

1) if you've decided to get up earlier to spend time with family before work or to eat healthier or get to work earlier, then make it of utmost importance and priority to do so

2) if you've decided to do the above, then you will likely need to go to bed earlier; decide what time to go to bed and follow through, not giving in to more reading, television, work, or computer time

3) if you've decided it would be good for you to make some dietary and exercise changes, then deliberately and slowly make those changes for yourself and your health

4) if you've decided to spend more "quality time" with your spouse or significant other, then arrange to do so rather than continuing the cycle of "hello/goodbye" living with them each day- practice LVAC with them

5) if you've decided to tackle a project at home or for your health, then list out the steps you'll need to follow to accomplish these things; make that appointment with your doctor, or visit the home

improvement store, or clear off your desk or kitchen table to get started paying those bills or doing the taxes

Again, deliberate living is very different from living reactively.

You'll experience more energy and greater self-esteem, you'll be more in line with who you really are and what you really want, and you'll free yourself from many of the internal and external struggles which bind you and cause you to need to escape from your life.

chapter

21 "Life is a Push-Mower"

You know, whenever I'm talking with someone, a patient of mine or otherwise, about the consistently challenging nature of life, this "Push Mower" analogy often comes up. I must say, it is not a particularly popular analogy, as it is a bit grim perhaps, and *very* hard to ignore.

Remember those old manual push mowers, also known as push reel mowers?

The ones I think about (and talk about with my patients) are the old style ones with the wooden bodies and steel blades that you'd have to push through the grass with enough force to cut it.

To my recollection, these were not easy machines to handle, complete with repeated snags on clumps of the lawn making them come to a sudden halt despite the amount of force you'd apply. In fact, it was the sudden and repeated stops that I remember best about these old machines.

The point here is that, time and time again, people will come in and tell me, quite sincerely and often while in much pain, all about how "stuck" they are in their lives.

I'll often discuss with them the "Stuff of Life" idea, as you may have read about earlier in this book, or maybe the "We Run, We Search" idea, or the "Deliberate Life" idea.

Yet, despite these discussions, and with all the honesty and sincerity in the world, people still often feel stuck and cannot get moving on things they know they need to or want to do for themselves and their lives.

This is when we'll start to talk about the "Life is a Push Mower" idea.

The way I picture it and describe it, if you look around you, you will truly see lots of folks who are sitting around with an imaginary old push mower sitting right next to them waiting for them to get up and push it.

Now some of my patients will tell me they'd really prefer that life be a gasoline or electric mower, preferably self-propelled, or better yet a riding mower.

But, for better or for worse, the fact remains that life, for most of us, really is more of a push power. That is, if we don't actually get up and push it along, the metal blades will NOT turn, and the grass will not get cut.

So, for example, if you are getting up on a particular day, and you've got a list of things you know you need to or want to do, there is no way to get around the fact that *you yourself actually have to put things into motion deliberately, and with focus and energy.*

There is no doubt that on that morning, you've got an imaginary old manual push mower leaning on the wall or the nightstand right next to you waiting for you to push it.

If you don't, it will be happy to keep leaning there next to you indefinitely as your lifetime goes by.

chapter

22 "Taking Ownership"

Certainly, you might *imagine* what a little chapter like this would be about, but likely you wouldn't guess it immediately.

While working extensively with people regarding the pain that they've gone through (and continue to go through) in their lives, often dating back to childhood disappointments and emotional betrayals by the important adults in their lives during those years, we often come to a certain wall eventually.

That is, as they struggle with past hurts, the person still finds it incredibly difficult to not be enraged or contemptuous towards their spouse or family of origin today.

So, for example, if we're talking about how a spouse disappoints them or pushes their buttons (see Chapter entitled "Marriage Part Two"), we'll eventually get stuck on the fact that they really and truly, no matter how consistently they try, still get very angry with the spouse and find it impossible to act in any other way except enraged, disgusted, or even contemptuous.

This is where the concept of "Taking Ownership" comes in.

It means, put simply, that eventually, in order to heal from the past, we must all stop expecting full and total retribution from people in our lives today for the hurts of the past, and take ownership of our pain and resentments ourselves.

Now, you may want to read that last sentence again.

I want to be sure to add here, that I *never* bring this topic up right away with people who I've just started working with.

First of all, everybody is different with regards to how deep their emotional wounds go and how able they are to live their lives as fully as possible with these wounds.

Secondly, it is never the first step to tell a person that they need to take ownership of their pain and "move on", etc., despite what people try to tell you about "getting over it", or "sucking it up", or "come on, that was thirty years ago". The thought alone makes me shudder, for it is impossible to simply forgive and forget.

No, this idea of taking ownership must be considered very carefully and with great and ι respect for people's pain and how difficult it is for any ur us to grasp the idea that we may never get fully compensated or considered for the extent of that suffering.

But the importance of this concept is that, generally speaking, only a rare person in your life will risk telling you honestly about it. And this only as a last step *after* they've Listened, Validated, Asked, and Commented over time (see Chapter entitled "LVAC".)

That's because the idea of "taking ownership" can sound so non-validating, and people will have anxiety about mentioning it to you for fear of hurting or angering you.

But, in fact, this step is not only NOT meant to further harm or insult, *it is meant to empower and to heal.*

Look at yourself in the mirror.

Tell yourself that, ultimately, after you've set appropriate boundaries and applied some of the ideas and techniques in this book towards yourself and towards others; that ultimately, your left-over anger, resentment, hostility, guilt, shame, fear, feelings of unfair treatment, etc., are yours and yours alone to reconcile.

If you don't, you will continue to try to exact your pound of flesh from the loved ones in your life, thus perpetuating these very feelings both in yourself and in them.

Again, this does *not* mean "forgive and forget", nor does it mean, "get over it and move on".

What it means is that we humans need FIRST to be heard and validated, encouraged to clarify our feelings, and given caring guidance and support.

THEN, eventually, we need to take ownership of the final, loose emotional ends in order to heal more fully and gain more personal power and satisfaction in our relationships.

I've really never seen true, comprehensive healing happen in any other way without this last step, immensely difficult as it can be.

chapter
23 "Kids and Happy Memories"

If there's a key phrase to keep at the forefront of your mind and heart when raising your children, it's this: "Make Happy Memories."

You may have heard other people say this, as I certainly have, both in and outside of my private office.

Nevertheless, I think it is worth a short discussion here since it is such a powerful, simple concept we all can use right away.

Time and time again people share with me vivid memories of parents becoming very angry or even abusive with them as children, or perhaps storming off in disgust with them or leaving in a huff after they did something wrong.

What I find remarkable though, is the people telling me these stories hardly ever actually remember the details of what the parent was actually angry about or what exactly they did to trigger the parent.

All they remember is the parent's actual behavior and how they were left feeling frightened, upset, worried, confused, sad, crushed, guilty, sorry, angry, etc.

The point here is that we as parents absolutely have great power in being able to lay down long-term memories in our children, both good and bad.

They will remember *how we made them feel, more than the details of what happened to trigger our reactions.*

Along these lines, it is also true that people, no matter how many upsetting or mixed memories they may have about a particular parent, can often also point out one or more "happy" memories involving them as well.

For example, the alcoholic, verbally abusive father who also taught his daughter how to change the oil in her car or chop wood. Or the depressive mother who was often locked away in her room and unavailable, but who also influenced her son's love of art and literature. And so it goes.

So, pick an activity, any activity, whether it's a simple walk around the block or nature path, sports, or perhaps sitting around playing games or music or just talking. Whatever you choose, you can look at this as a part of your parenting of them which is pretty much guaranteed to help their overall memory of you in the long run, as well as their overall emotional development.

And, believe me, these "Happy Memories" also do count quite a bit in their overall image of themselves and the world later on, as I observe in my office everyday in the adults I converse with.

chapter
24 "The Boiling Pot and the Lid"

A very simple idea here, yet one which many people find useful and helpful: teenagers, and even some pre- and post-teens, are like boiling pots of water and we the parents are like the lids that go on the pots.

It is quite literally their job to push the limits, or, in other words, *to try to throw the lid off of themselves as they boil.*

It is our job not to be thrown off completely.

Trust me when I say, your child, no matter how much he or she tells you to leave them alone, or how much they try to hide things from you, does NOT want you to give up on them. They WANT the lid to stay on. They NEED the lid.

A patient of mine told me that his parents once called the police on him and had him taken away, even though the responding police officers recommended against it. Another man shared that his parents ultimately stopped checking up on his drinking and staying out late. Yet another told me about how his parents told him that he was allowed to smoke marijuana since they did it when they were his age.

What these three men also ultimately concluded was that they were disappointed in their parents, and that they faced greater challenges and consequences in their lives than they felt they would have faced otherwise, had things been different back then. They felt like they had thrown the lid off the pot.

Put simply, *we cannot necessarily win each battle with our adolescent children, but, ultimately, we can outlast them.*

As long as we know this, we can at least know that we are *limiting* the damage by realizing that the goal is not to make things nice and tidy; ie. your kid may still experiment with drugs or alcohol or sex, but probably not to the extent they would have had you given up on them just because it seemed so impossible to win completely.

Keep in mind that, by the time your child is a teenager, or even a pre-teen, you've already faced at least one other period of time when they've tested your limits: remember the "terrible twos"?

Well, briefly, between the ages of 24 to 36 months of age, our children are experimenting for the first time with independence from us on a smaller scale. They need limits, but they also need our unconditional positive regard and empathy.

Your teen, pre-teen, or recently-post-teen child is the same way, only bigger and can do more harm to themselves while going through this phase.

They'll still need your unconditional positive regard and empathy, and, though they don't know it yet, they really do need to NOT be able to throw the lid off the boiling pot.

To visit Dr. Ferraioli online, go to:

www.drferraioli.com

Made in the USA
Middletown, DE
11 November 2015